The Gifted Power of Women,

Yesterday,

and

Forever.

JEAN BELIZAIRE

Author & Pastor

Books Academy LLC
112 SW H K Dodgen Loop,
Temple, Texas 76504
Hotline: (254) 800-1189

Ordering Information:
Quantity sales. Special discounts are available on quantity purchases by corporations, associations, and others. For details, contact the publisher at the address above.

Printed in the United States of America.

ISBN-13:   Softcover   978-1-966567-40-0
              eBook   978-1-966567-41-7

Library of Congress Control Number:

Dedication Page

This book is dedicated to Loretta Weaver, my nana and God mother who has been there for me from my youth and into my adulthood. I appreciate her loving strength and her care throughout the years and I pray women all across the world learn to be like her. I love you, Nana!

Introduction

Women all across the world are being devalued, and feeling oppression and suppression. Yet they still remain the queens of the world we live in. Come and journey with me into both the plight and significance of women in the world today. Let us praise them for their strength and their inherent beauty and recognize God's reasons for making—women.

Chapter 1
I Need Only What You Can Give

Have you ever considered the existence of women? Have you ever gone far beyond skin deep beauty to figure find the specialness that lives in each and every single woman? Have you ever thought about God, the divine, or the universes' active role in the creation of the female sex?

This book is some musing on that. The hummingbird is a powerful bird its wings move in rapidity as it fiercely makes it to its goal. It's an ambition or desire is to surface sweet nectar from the very depths of plant life. Its beak is long and extended far enough to extract nectar from the beautifully and colored array of various plants…

The term Wanganeges is a Haitian Creole term to define the hummingbird and in Haiti, there are so many of them flying through the humidity-filled air where its residents are scorched daily by the sun's heat. Haiti is known for its black magic and the term "wanga" is used for declaring various love spells casted by a lover onto the loved to make them fall for them in an unnatural way.

This book is not about black magic or how you can conjure favor from spirits to cause a lover to be loyal to you or to fix a relationship problem. This book is, however, about the magic of women how after all these years on planet Earth there remains, whether you believe in a creation story or the Big Bang, that the existence of women is a very strong and keen influence on mankind…

The very first encounter with a woman we see Adam in need of a companion, how the Bible records state that he was in paradise on earth, and in this earthly paradise he suffered a lack but did not know what or who it was he was missing. And how the divine being we know as " God " put him into a deep sleep leading him to a heightened ecstasy and from within him produced a woman from his rib cage and presented to him, not a girlfriend, or a date but a wife ...

God had put the woman in man but drew her out by way of a deep sleep and made her an individual with the great capacity and also, she too was morally and physically perfect as Adam was. Was it sex that Adam needed? Was it the ability to procreate and raise sons and daughters that he needed? Was it help to till the vast paradise known as the Garden of Eden?

I challenge you the reader in saying no, but he did need someone or something like her for himself. Now there are people who live single and live single comfortably and successfully however, a majority of men can't live single the need for a woman exists. But do they even understand their own need? What is it that they want? Do they really know?

I challenge one to say that it is deeper than sex although the first time Adam and Eve had sex it was not tainted by the things that are so prevalent in today's society such as lack of faithfulness, social media, pornography, and the like. Their sex life was special I imagine and we live today to have what they had in a relationship however, we don't come close because of moral failings.

I believe that there were unique qualities in only found in Eve that God made gender-specific and personality-specific to Eve... Remember, Eve never crawled as a baby, she never went through puberty, she was a total and complete living soul without having the phases of humanity that we have. Adam too be was made a man from the start and not a child, teenager, adolescent, etc.

He was made a fully grown man but even though fully grown with muscles and many features he was lacking because he needed a female version of himself. One that was like him but feminine in sex, feminine in soul, and feminine in mind. And Adam needed what the animal kingdom had maleness and femaleness but he had not that for himself. And neither could he provide that for himself...

God extracted a woman out of his rib, the rib was created to guard the heart to protect internal organs and with that protection, he made a life using the ingredients of a rib cage to produce a woman. And this woman was Eve, the mother of all the living.

Today there is a problem in society. People are together but not together like Adam and Eve were. People hold hands and walk in the park but the intimacy is different now than what it was back then. Because the world we now live in is shattered and bruised by sin and all types of chaotic behavior.

If we believe that the Bible record is true about the first humans on the earth, then paradise was once here, and this planet was a perfect place, and everything in it was perfect. This means there was no moral flaw to contend with. We mostly talk of their fall but not so much what they fell from...

And woman today although flawed are still God's gift to man. Is there such a thing as the right woman for the right man? Are women seen more as objects of desire rather than lifetime companions? And If so, why is that? Is it the culture, television, movies, or just plain lack of knowledge that leads to them being objects of the hormonal instincts of men...?

Are women approaching relationships wrong or is it the men or both of them? If you are a man and you are reading this book then you should know that most times if not all the time, we are approaching women wrong and that the woman need education on how they should be approached as well.

Chapter 2
Culture is Charged with Killing The Role of Women

No country is as filled with culture and the effects of it as is the United States of America. It is true that culture is a worldwide thing and that culture is part of our fabric as we know it today. And although it's good to be familiar with culture sometimes the trends and ways of the world need to be confronted.

I remember on the night of my ordination I was charged by a beloved friend to "confront the culture" and that a reference to John the Baptist and his boldness in confronting Herod about having his brother's wife was used to charge me to not fit into the molds of common day culture and to inspire a culture of Christ in this world order of things.

Women live in a sex crazed culture sex is put up first before getting to know a woman. One is prodded to look at shapes and sizes, images of how a woman should dress and look dominate the television screens and magazines. Music such as that of gangsta rap portrays women as beings who desire the glamour and glitz of the wealthy life. Woman are portrayed as" thot" an idea of sexual pleasure. If you are African American then your rear end and breast must be big, if you are Caucasian then you must be blonde and thin...

Woman are so image-conscious they try everything from the gym to various diets to fit the mold, some have to deal with the drug culture as well and there is music that makes them feel they must be ok with narcotics and pills to have a good time or a good life. Sometimes women are confused about what type of man to choose, settling for the same experience as the last, just with a different face. So, they are not uniquely in love.

Manhood is programmed into their consciousness as a certain type of way making it difficult for some to ever be married. I remember meeting a very beautiful African American woman at community organizing retreat in Apple Gate, California. We were to interview each other to discover how we both got involved in this line of work.

It was a group activity I would always remember. The woman asked me where I was from and I told her the Boston area and she said wow you sound like you are from New York and I love New York I was honored by her intrigue in talking to me. She asked me if I was married and I replied no, that I was waiting on the Lord for a wife and she replied that she was married and was finding it hard to find a strong man like her father.

She mentioned her father was her track coach and the epitome of manhood to her and that she met many guys but all of them too weak to be with her. I told her she might be blocking her blessing if she weeds out men based on how her father is. At time that I write this I wonder if she ever met the man she wanted since that meeting was sometime in 2011. However, I sat that to say some women have a poor point of reference to go bye, or maybe just too much expectations to be married.

Marriage has certainly come under attack and scrutiny and this culture does not you hold the standards of a committed love by far. Woman are misguided in what they are looking for and in how they should be. Sex without intimacy is what they experience. And they did not realize some of whom they should be to a man because Satan has polluted the airwaves with subliminal messages that kill their role and expectations.

And not too many are exposed to a good spiritual teaching of their God-given and ordained role as the female sex, and feminine soul that they are. Today there are a lot of hurt and angry women because Satan has attacked them and belittled their importance reducing themselves to sexual objects and maternal beings.

But there is so much to a woman and we shall discover that the Lord meant for it to be an awesome journey to know them. And that every woman in essence is beautiful. And wonderfully made.

Chapter 3
Enter the Matrix of Womanhood

I recall a song by an R&B group called Escape entitled "Understanding" and in the song, the women were expressing the need for understanding, not agreement but understanding. Today world is filled with misunderstanding however women have long since been misunderstood. And to be honest some women are in the process of understanding themselves.

Women are a matrix; however, I propose love as a means to understanding them it seems that women are wired that way to respond to love but there are different types of love. The love they may get from a child that they have nurtured and loved is very different from the love they may get from a man they parented that child with.

Women are more verbose than man, from childhood they communicate more words than a male child, they mature before men a man may not mature until later in life. I believe that they mature quicker because they have the unique responsibility of being future mothers, they are on a biological that ticks while they seek to find a masculine man to mate and raise a family with.

Women think differently than men, they are aroused to sexual intimacy by how they are treated while men are more visual and need to only see a woman that is to their liking to be aroused.

Love is the unconditional acceptance of someone it is not that one condones wrongdoing but that your love for them remains in the best interest of that person, your love doesn't quit in the face of a moral failure but it burns with passion and remains firm in testing.

This is how to understand the matrix of women. They have PMS and cannot be at peace with themselves during that time because they have not reached the goal of being impregnated and the physical happenstances take their toll on them, physically, emotionally, and psychologically.

But how does one arrive at love? Love is not planned all the time; love can come by way of an occasion but unconditional love is intentional. It is an act that comes with one's mind towards a person. And this intent is reemphasized daily making someone committed to the object of their love. Therefore, one is able to both enter and understand the matrix of a woman.

Chapter 4
Ones Searching for Love

So, are men really looking for love? Or are they looking for sex? And how does the manner of their search affect a woman? I once discovered a song by Damian "Junior Gong" Marley the son of Bob "Gong" Marley. It was a song that was created when he was about 16 years old and it was entitled "Searching".

And in the song, he talks about his daily search for love. The maturity and creativeness of the song spoke clearly of his gifting and future success with his musical career. Why are men so sex driven? Why is it that men are dubbed as dogs who cannot stay in a monogamous relationship?

Some of it is a man's nature to be a pursuer of a woman. The problem is that in the pursuit of a woman, one's focus becomes his hormonal leading. Men do struggle with lust and for some men, it's not a struggle it's a desire they constantly give in to making it a lifestyle. Woman want to be loved. I've heard it said that this is why they become sexual, to begin with.

If all men are pursuing sex and sex alone, then women can't expect love because sex is what men are searching for so this impacts women greatly but the love factor is not a one-sided thing because men are wired for love too. I propose that we are created so. However, men battle trust issues with women, making it difficult to love because they come into a relationship with the idea that a woman is a bitch.

If the man's perspective of a woman can change then he is free and open to love and this impacts a woman greatly because he is not guarded to the point of being aloof to her, seeking only a time in the sheets with her but he would be valuing her and loving her in masculine way and she would love him according to her femininity.

Love is a word that exists on our vocabulary, however, is all too often not experienced in the true sense of the word because the times have made love foreign to us. People can get married, have a child, purchase a home together, and can never be in love. True love that is. We live today in a very loveless society. Can this society improve? Why is love important? Does it produce anything? The answer to the latter question is that it can produce.

Love produces a mass production of things when arrived at and firmly set. When there is mutual love between a man and a woman one enters into how things are created to be. Purposes and intents are clear and the beautiful relationship manifests itself.

Women want to be loved in a masculine way. They are looking for that, they are searching and yearning for this experience, and some when they cannot find it give up hope and this is where same sex relationships begin to exist with women.

Until they can be loved in a masculine way they can never feel or be fulfilled.

Chapter 5
The Prototype

The term "daddy's little girl" we are all fond of we hear it in music that is played, we read about it in magazines, we use the cliche or term in conversation. However, do we really grasp the meaning of this? Is there something intrinsic about being a daughter to a father that differs from being a son to a father?

Sons are usually treated with a toughness that sometimes can be too much, if it is a healthy balance between love and discipline, they will make out okay. If they are too heavy-handed on their son then there will be resentment and a lack of communication. However, daughters hold a special place in a father's heart because most fathers become their protectors.

The idea that something would happen to a father's daughter terrifies them and they would go to any length to guard them and shelter them from life's storms and men that seek to break their daughter's heart. So, women need protection from a man they need to feel safe just they did with their dad. And when their dad is gone a sense of security from this cold world is missing.

They are in search for a prototype of protection. They need to not feel nervous around a man, to be able to be themselves and feel safe. An outlet to communicate their emotions without judgment. I've met women who are abused by a man and that seek shelter from their dad towards a significant other who is mistreating them.

I once dated a girl who was abused for 18 years of her life by her children's father, she was exposed to drug dealing and drug use. She was closer to her dad than she was her mother. Her dad died and she continued on with the resiliency she had but every time around the anniversary of his death it was a tough time for her. It was the courts that could provide protection for her, or a restraining order, or a new man it was from the man she knew really loved her. And with him passing on it made it so that she could not experience his protective love and she felt lost because of it.

She needed a carbon copy of her father. She needed a man that could be that fine- tuned machine of strength for her all the time, she needed a man that was interested in her without just an interest in sex. She needs protection for her three kids and shelter and covering from danger...

This is what a woman, a healthy woman mentally and emotionally needs from a man. And there are those that don't realize what they need and ping pong from one man to another short changing themselves out of dignity and respect because internally they are confused and damaged. Even traumatized and stricken with low self-esteem.

Chapter 6
No Contest

I once was a pastor at a small church in New Bedford, Massachusetts and one day I was on the from steps of the church waiting for a Bible study to begin, as I observed a very beautiful woman walking down the street. And someone who was there with me said "Sometimes a woman's beauty is a gift and a curse".

It's funny because some women who are drop-dead gorgeous find themselves to be ugly, yet in the eyes of others, they are beautiful. Where does the low self-esteem come from? Was it something someone said? Or something someone did? What made them so insecure to begin with? Do they need therapy? Could they use a motivational book or talk?

The questions are limitless, and the answers are unsearchable. Some women won't admit to the insecurity they just keep the thought floating around in their heads.There is a sense of competition if they are with someone, they may feel at times like they are competing for someone's love and affection, when they are out with their boyfriend or husband and see they eyeing another woman's body, this creates or adds to their insecurity...

They wonder if they are enough and if their significant other is satisfied with just being with them. Sometimes the insecurity comes from their family unit and how they were brought up. Sometimes it's because they haven't arrived at being pregnant and their biological clock is ticking. Or maybe they desire to be married and maybe they are one of single person's in their household that never found a man to commit to them on that level, they just were on the status of a girlfriend, booty call, friends with benefits, one night stand etc.

Women are in constant competition with themselves and others. It's when they realize their uniqueness in God that they set aside the need and want for a contest.

Chapter 7
Fragile, Handle With Care

I have found in my life and my experience with dating that I've attracted many abused women. The question is why? What is it about me that I have attracted them? Or is it the fact that most women are suppressed, oppressed, and abused? And if it is that most women experience abuse, how did they become victims, and are they honest with themselves about it?

I've discovered that some nice guys attract abused women and that it is something in that guy that they long for, an ideal relationship that they see however, they are not really ready for because they have never come to terms with being victims of abuse. They just attribute the abuse to their abuser's ways, or to culture, or even as their fault...

Why do men abuse women? And are they being a real man when they do so? Seems like they are not real men in the truest sense of the word however they have both believed and learned that this is the way to solve something they are angry about. How can they say in one breath " I love you " and then backhand a woman or call her a name that demotes her?

Women respond to love yet some have settled for being unloved in their relationship. I once dated a woman that was with her abuser for 18 years. She told me that he had only tried to hit her once deep in my heart and mind I knew it was more than that. As we progressed in our newfound relationship, I realized it was way more than that, that she had settled for severe dysfunction... To the point where she never had sought out help until she had started to deal with me...

Women are strong and vibrant spirits yet fragile and to be handled with Care at the very same time. What I mean is that there is a balance to how much they can handle and how much they can or should take. Now, relationships is tricky because it's working through things, communicating, having patience, listening, compromising on some things, and taking a stand on things.

Women have been known across the ages to be the weaker sex physically. They do not have muscle or brawn. And they do not have certain job positions because of that. However intellectually they are stronger and emotionally more secure to share their feelings, and intuitively they have instincts that reign supreme!

But they still need care and care is not just a heartfelt thing. It is a thing a man must practice and practice leads to perfection! How does a man care for a woman? And at one point does it become too much, if there is such a thing?

Seems like in the culture, particularly the black culture men are taught not to care for a woman, and to disregard her as a spiritual being that is beside him. And that this lack of care is ingrained in the black man. It seems that most n

Men let their libido guide them into multi relationships and women settle for these kinds of guys feeling that they are truly alpha males. But what is an alpha male versus a beta male?

I used to talk to friends who felt they were a beta male and read articles on themselves that criticized them saying that the nice guy always finished in last place and that women inherently chose the alpha male and rejected the beta male being attracted to the testosterone of the supposed alpha male....

The fact is that all men have testosterone and we must distinguish between what is culture and upbringing versus what is inherent.

Chapter 8
Spiritually, Do Women Have A Place?

I read a book some time ago, called "Why men hate going to church" I can't recall the author at this time... The book was basically discussing a woman's role in church versus a man's role in church and why men have a hard time finding a place in the very feminized church communities that exist...

But the question really goes do women really have a place in church? It's true that inner-city churches churches have many women that attend. They have faithful attendees from all over. However, if women are not fully embraced in the secular world what would make you think that they would be embraced in church? Yes, in church there is supposed to be love and equality but that's not always the case ...

For example, the church has long been divided on whether women should be in leadership ... I have heard preachers tout from the Bible reasons why women shouldn't even so much as speak in the church ... And some of this comes from the Bible and Pauline Epistles that sometimes don't make sense.

However the church has been more culture-seeking and some denominations embrace women pastors, prophetesses, etc... but still women sometimes feel unheard and without a voice... So, what's the problem?

The answers lie in a male-dominated creation that do not applaud, the powers of women but women's power have their place.

First of all, it is my belief that God ordains who shall be what they shall be; it is he that ordains whether you are male or female, and that goes according to his plan for your life. Have you ever stopped and wondered why you are who you are? Came from the family you came from? Been through what you been through? Every finite detail is included in your blueprint for your life...

And it makes sense to consult God for your proper place, of in fact God speaks and God cares then will he guide us into his master plan? The answer is a resounding, yes!

So, women are powerful and do have a powerful place in life they are not just here to nurture and to emote feelings but the same anointing that endows men, when they come to God, anoints them to live and so the task that's necessary can be fulfilled completely and without delay.

Women have a proper spiritual place and physical, emotional, and psychological role to play on life besides becoming sex objects and groomers of children.

They have God almighty, El Shaddai in them, and that speaks for itself.

Chapter 9
What Are Women Looking For, Do They Know?

They say that women mature faster than a man, they speak more words and they see life from a different world view. This could be because they are hard-wired to raise a family and genetically they are inclined to be that way at a young age ..

They say that women are attracted to testosterone in men testosterone is that chemical that makes a man strong. So they are looking for strength but strength for what? I feel that men are natural-born leaders and that men are to lead their families, at this time however family breaks up are at an all-time high so the question is asked what is happening to the men? Why are they leaving their families or why are there so many cases in court for child support? Why are they fathering children from afar if they are ever really fathering at all?

There seems to be something spiritual going on where families are made and broken, particularly in the minority community. Children are raised without a father and mothers are left to play the role of both mother and father to a curious child who wonders why are they alone all the time. Why is there an attack or a case of this among the working poor? My guess is because they are already down so why not destroy them?

Families that have money don't readily have this problem, so does money keep relationships alive? I say that money surely keeps children provided for, so the rich and wealthy use that to make up for the personal qualities needed to raise a healthy family, but money can't buy love, as the Beatles once sang, and this is very, very true. Women are looking to be loved, but the culture is countering that. Love is that indestructible force that makes a difference in the lives of others, it's so very powerful that it dispels darkness and wars and builds a house a house that will be a home but many houses are not homes but atmospheres of rage and anger and discontent.

Religion teaches love but it's perfected in a real-life circumstance that is imperfect and very flawed so women are genetically attracted to testosterone but the deeper thing is love but if a man does not know God he cannot love, the only thing he can do is lust for her and that is as superficial as things can get.

Because beauty is fleeting ... And so fleeting that an outside partnership is sure to ensue. Men cheat more than women and women cheat too just not always in the same way. Some cheat emotionally, and mentally before it becomes physical. While men cheat physically and repeatedly as life goes by.

It is not about sex but it's made to be about that. And when the reality of life settles in and children are made and born this is where the test of strength comes in ..so women do know what they want. If they are mature and spiritually healthy psychologically and emotionally healthy too they will surely have an aim with things...

So, do men have an aim? Are they really men because they are physically developed? Do they need to be taught to a for family or are their lust an aim to destroy what God created which is a family unit?

Chapter 10
Love And Race, Race And Love

.So The race thing is very interesting there are more interracial relationships in existence than ever. White women are with black men, black women are worth white men etc. And when we see these things in public it is a shock to our personal culture and values...

Sometimes it manifests our own prejudices and biases and the ugliness of our hearts shows itself to ourselves and we must sit down and reflect on where it's coming from and we must ask ourselves if we are really as loving and people-oriented as we say we are.

Back in the Civil Rights era, it was taboo to say that we are in such relationships and some faced lynching of Klansmen for it today you can see someone walking down the streets with their companion or on the bus with their lovers and it's all commonplace.

But there are still problems with such relationships sometimes it comes from family other times it's from close friends. The idea of being with your own and making babies with your own still dominates most thinking. Even me, when I see a black woman with a white man it makes me wonder what reasons with that woman gives to be with that man...

We are open more today with our love and I've had white girlfriends and lovers. And some I miss today wondering how they are doing and how life is for them since we broke up..............Is it right to have an interracial relationship or is it wrong? I believe that love is blind and it does not see color. Unfortunately, with racial tensions up high due to police brutality and such that some people may hide their love.

Love is a powerful virtue and the biases of race disappear when and where true love exists. But how many people are in love today with their significant other? Or are they just with someone because they are afraid of being alone?

No one wants to be alone unless they choose celibacy as an option for living but that is few and very far between. Women have to be bold these days about such occurrences in their life and racial tensions and pressure affect their decision making.

If they have kids with someone of another race, they have to explain the interracial connection to their kids and their kids' lives with the pressure from friends and classmates, and even adults who disapprove of such love...

Identity crises ensue and some may either develop positively or negatively in such circumstances some may develop with a positive worldview and may embrace an interracial relationship as they get older because they grew up in such homes.

Needless to say, it's a difficult undertaking the more committed a women gets but it may produce beautiful results if they are able to navigate the waters of that interracial love well enough to get to a peaceful shore.

Chapter 11
Miss Moneybags

Financial security is needed by all of us, however, when a woman expresses it in a relationship it's an issue or they are seen as money-hungry gold diggers. The truth of the matter is that women need to feel safe. And that they do not want to go on a wild roller coaster ride with a broken man.

My observation is that a man that is food with money communicates good leadership to a woman, leadership that she can trust and follow otherwise she cannot respect that man. He may be good at lovemaking and she may even have his children but she will never respect him because his lack of financial government and management communicates that he does not care about her or her family.

Money is an amoral thing. It's neither good nor bad it's good you use it and what lengths that you are willing to go to for it that comes under scrutiny. Some people will kill for money, others will lie and cheat for it as well. And these things are frowned upon but why is money so important to women and their relationship as well?

If a man is just talking to women, then money is not involved but once there is a commitment to each other than one's values and beliefs about money come into play strongly. If their values are not balanced then, one may save money and make it work for them and the other may not.

It's especially important to deal with debt before getting married or buying a house debt in a relationship can hinder Harmony and forward progress. It can cause arguments over finding a happy medium about things it can frustrate a couple and even lead to divorce. Frivolous spending that you can't afford to do can hinder financial success...

Once values are taught to them consciously and subconsciously a person may not even see their values towards money unless get into a counselor's office and they can see the errors they have committed. And sometimes they may go flat broke and then look back in hindsight to miss appropriating their funds and such...

So, are women Golddiggers? Some are but most aren't they just worry about a future that's stable. They mature quicker than men so they know how much money is key to a family dynamic. A man that has his act together promotes a woman to confidence and communicates self-discipline whereas a broke man communicates foolishness and the lack of understanding that money is essential and vital to life - period...

Some men spend on women and some don't today's culture promotes that one doesn't spend on a significant other as if it's a sign of strength... there is such a thing as a sugar daddy and that is not respected by women even when the money is being spent on them. They may accept but they will not respect...

A good Steward of the money God has blessed a man with will be rewarded. Of course, there are emergencies and unexpected spending but a man who wastes his money has wasted all his time working for it and obtaining it.

So, when should this be discussed well, if you are getting married to someone it should be discussed before marriage. And if you are not married but find yourself deeply involved it should be talked about as soon as circumstances arise when you start spending...

If you are single then the upside to that is you don't have the same expectations as a couple does so you can save tremendously but if you find yourself seeing someone than, it can alter your lifestyle and you should talk it out and come to some resolve ...

Money is a bartering system that woman understand they see the need to survive and to do so for family's sake, they may even feel like part of a team or loved because you can manage money and make money now money will never buy affection and passionate love but money will help your future and give you options that a broke couple won't have and, to be honest, if your money game isn't straight, you should not even be in a relationship of any kind.

Chapter 12
It's A Mind Thing

The saying that things are mind over matter rings true, but what is it like to have the mind of a woman? And how does it differ from the mind of a man? The subject of maturity comes up in examining this because woman go through puberty before men and woman use a different hemisphere of their mind than men do
.

So how do you attract a woman if you are a man seeking a relationship? I think you have to win over their mind and this is a continuous effort. Woman are into a man's looks but not as much as a man is into the looks of a woman. A man can be unappealing in his looks and win over a super model but why is this a continuous effort? It's because very few men seek to win over a woman mentally but their mind is where the real attraction is created.

Men have to be able to connect with women and this is hard if one can't listen and pay attention and understand them as they express themselves. A woman is always emoting and sharing her feelings which are based in their thoughts because thoughts produce feelings but if you can't capture her thoughts, you cannot capture her feelings.

But most men do not care about this game of thrones, the way to master a woman is to connect with her thought life which is ever-changing and evolving that is why it doesn't matter how great of a lover you are in bed, you can't keep her I'd you can't love her mind and make love to her mind which is the essence of her being and this is a lifelong effort, especially in a marriage where you vow to be together in a public ceremony forever...

What's important to a man contrast in what is important to a woman. And you don't have to learn to think like a woman if you are a man you just have to learn to let them know that you care about their thoughts and see where they are coming from... but this is a moment-by-moment thing and not a one-and-done effort.

Men are not very communicative as a woman; they have not learned the art of conversation. It could be that they had a problem in their upbringing, or maybe their personal development was poor. May they haven't been applying themselves to the art and mastery of winning a woman over in her mind.

It's what you say, and what you do that aligns you with the soul of a woman and it's not necessarily in the gifts you but her or the money you give her that she is one because she could view those things in a negative light if you are not careful to love her...

It's a mind thing woman know how they feel about things. And they learn to think intuitively it's a survival thing and it's always at play even when surviving a relationship with a man. So it's your mind connect connecting with hers and finding a level ground that makes you effective in keeping her soul aligned with yours it's not the way you make love, although that is part of it, or the gifts you buy it's mastering her mind that key and this is a constant effort.

Chapter 13
Why Some Women Become Lesbian

I have dated a woman that had a history of bisexuality and as a man I was worried about being cheated on. I figured if this woman wanted to cheat one me with another woman, she could and I would never know it. Because man who is dating a woman that is professing to be hetero sexual you never think of them as cheating on you with another woman but another man ...

I have to say that when I started to date these woman it was not known to me about their lesbian desires but something I found out by happenstance. It troubled me nevertheless but of course, the times I dated them I was Leary about being with them. And I was not in a good space spiritually.

So, what did I learn from them? I learned that they left the usage of men for the same sex because they hated men, and they were dissatisfied with men and concluded that they were all the same. Yes, they had a sexual impulse that was burning, but that wasn't just the driving force the thing was men had failed them, didn't understand them, were never going to be good to them, so they figured they hated men and loved women like them who also were disgruntled with men...

Some of them had kids so there was confusion like whose the Daddy and such is it a man or another woman. Recently the educational world was trying to include same- sex relationships in school curriculum. They were seeking to be in tune with today's culture and some real-life situations that exist. Confusion was and is a given and sometimes these lesbian and same-sex relationships become toxic. Just as toxic for a woman as if they were dating a man.

What are woman trying to communicate when they become lesbian? Is it just the need for another female body? Or is there a deeper reason? I say that there is a deeper psychological reason why they are involved with another woman. Some leave the usage of men altogether and some, like the women I dated still see men but find more understanding and love in another woman...

Men need to learn that in order not to lose your woman to another woman they have to learn how to purely love their woman God's way. And only God can teach and how to love his woman and be different than the other guys. He has to learn how to be in a class of his own.

Chapter 14
Love, Life, and Marriage

As a former pastor, I conducted rededication of marriages and newly said vows. I can't begin to express how much baggage comes in with when they marry others in holy matrimony. Now it's inevitable that people come into marriages sometimes with great debt, kids from other relationships, and certain scenarios and situations that can cripple their desire for a lifelong love.

It's not about the cost of the rings or the cost of the wedding that is an issue it's about the cost or price they will pay if they do not enter the marriage understanding what is expected of them when they do exchange vows before a public audience and embark on what is supposed to be a life long journey ...

Women dream and talk of marriage ever since they could remember and men walk into it by happenstance. It's important that people understand the spiritual aspect of marriage and that they are properly counseled heading in but some couples just use or need the minister to put them together but they are not together spiritually to endure the storms ahead.

So, what's the point of marriage today anyway? Is it just that we are enamored with being someone's one and only? It's deeper than that marriage goes back to Adam and Eve according to the Bible, God gave Eve to Adam there was not an exchange of vows, there was no public ceremony, there was no pastor to conduct a service. God conducted the service.

God created Eve from a rib as Adam was in a state of ecstasy and Adam recognized her as being like him, she was the feminine physical and he was the masculine physical and their natures were not alike but they were human and in paradise. As I write this it blows my mind that they were in paradise on earth and that nothing could've satisfied Adam in all the earth but the feminine physical of his own self. But he did not know what he needed but God knew, and provided that in the woman.

It was a union that meant something spiritually it was the union just did not mean something through the sexual union it meant something before God and to each other beautifully in their souls...

Some have debated whether there is such a thing as a soulmate, I have even challenged that idea or notion but as I write this write now, I realize that she was a soul mate to Adam, they would face everything together, they were as right as Bonnie and Clyde except in a good way.

Today's woman faces a challenge because men are not in search of a soul mate but sex partner for a moment's time. We live in a culture where most people are okay with living with each other and making babies. And they do not have God at the center of their love.

God was an important part of Adam's union, God played doctor and performed surgery on Adam, he was the love doctor in fact, only God could've done what was done. The culture is a disappointment for women, and they must learn what to accept and not accept. Divorce is high, and cases of child support for women who have been jaded are through the roof. Some women are playing the role of mother and father to children...

Abortion is high because they do not see men they are with as being a support and finances are an issue as well and so babies are aborted. Recently in the news, a baby was given birth to and found in the trash crying. The mother stated she thought the child was dead and that she had no finances for the baby. She was charged with attempted murder of her child. The interesting part of her statement to authorities was that she said she had nothing for the baby.

Women after giving birth suffer from postpartum and end up abusing their children, the men are not there to support. So where are the men? Sadly they are missing because they don't learn to desire family and to raise one. A lot of babies are born by accident. Maybe they had unprotected sex and got into the lovemaking only to produce a child they did not want with that person...
At this juncture, I have to confess that one time I laid with a woman out of sheer pleasure, and when she called me to tell me that she may

be pregnant I was not of the disposition to have her in particular as a my baby mother. I thought she was attractive enough to be with me sexually but not attractive enough for me to raise a family with. She ended up not being pregnant but I realized something ... I realized that I wasn't that committed to her and she probably wasn't that committed to me .. This is the culture we live in.

Chapter 15
Woman And The Workforce

Women and the workforce has been a long debated subject. Women are not viewed as men, and most jobs cater to men and not to women. Even with an education and more experience who pale in comparison to men. They run into a difficult time to find jobs. Sometimes if they are attractive enough their sex appeal may get them in but it may not be long before they are propositioned or harassed sexually....

Because they lack the physical capacity of a man by nature they cannot compete in jobs that are requiring or brawn if they are of great mental strength they are too intimating to follow and when I a position of power it's hard for them to have Co- workers that are male and will submit to their leadership.

Women have more emotional intelligence than men because they have intuition and can relate easily to others. They also can solve problems easier in a less aggressive way and come to a happy medium. Whereas men have a lot of testosterone involved in solving problems which makes them less successful in solving conflict than women.

Anal retentive women are woman that have a tough exterior but highly sensitive inward they can give off the impression of being sassy or strong which they are but they may not handle criticism well and disagreements well this has been my experience with women in church that I have met along the way.

Women are making strides in the work world but are still the subject of sexual aggression. So when will this change? Will it ever? The answer is there is always a difference between men and woman but although things may improve the difference in men and women shows in the work world and beyond.

Even with education, they are still low on the totem pole it seems as if they are only good for sex and babies and inferior to men who may pale in comparison to them. To be honest some women are very qualified when applying for work, very educated and capable but they take a backseat to sexist perspectives...

Even women in church that work as pastors, prophetesses, and deaconesses are victims of age-old sexism which diminishes their gifts and roles as not being as powerful as a man's. It kind of makes you question the roles of woman that are stated in the Bible. Are they sexist? Are they subject to the old world and it's way of thinking?

Will this change or will it remain the same? Did God create such a difference in man and woman that it will always impact women who seek high pay scales at jobs? It seems like the woman with the entrepreneurial spirit fairs better because she works for herself and takes matters into her own hands. And is in control of her own destiny.

Chapter 16
A Woman's Troubles

So we all know that a woman's menstruation period is a difficult time in her life. Because she is looking to get pregnant and is fighting against her biological clock. And my I qualify my statements to say not all women desire children but they know that If they should they are against time or fighting against time ...

I recall a conversation I had by phone with a female friend she was headed into her thirties and was not married yet and had no children she was pressed in the conversation because she had not yet met the man of her dreams and she did not have children yet. I tried to encourage her. She was very beautiful and could be with anyone she wanted to be with but was not yet in her season to be married.

She finally met someone, he wasn't a Christian like her but she loved him and they had a child together and she was a happy and very successful woman. I'd say all that to say it's hard to be a woman and they deserve our respect. Men in particular should respect women and some of their trouble is the lack of respect that comes from men...

Women, by nature, are strong-minded because they live in a world that throws a lot at them. Pressure comes from every hand, yet they still find the peaceful shores they are looking for or they strive for the peaceful shores they dream of...

Men have it easier than women yet respect is lacking. I have to say that I'm constantly learning to respect women. It's not that I'm a man of no regard it's that I have to understand the constant issues they face in order to esteem their strength, wisdom, and beauty. A woman is filled with troubles they learn young that men love sex, and they learn early that men desire to be with them in that way. However, they learn later in life the powers given to them by God.

Some of them never obtain spirituality which makes the journey even more difficult because they are body, soul, and spirit. And they may feed body and soul but may have no knowledge to fill their spirit. Sometimes they meet a godly man that can teach them and they fall into their rightful place in God and sometimes godly men are lacking so they don't get that from a man but they get that from another woman that can reach them from a woman's perspective

That's another thing too, the Bible is taught from different views and interpretations so they may not get the right view depending on who they are listening to. They need to nurture body and soul and spirit and that's a task in and of itself. It's not just a woman thing it's A God thing.

Chapter 17
I Need Meaning

Women crave meaning, a lot of relationships are unfulfilling. Sexual attraction is not ever enough to satisfy the soul of a woman. Because her soul is wired to be to live in love. The physical appearance of a man may pull her in but it's the love that will keep her and excite her.

Sex is a turn on but before she makes good love she must be loved and this is an art that men in today's society does not understand. So much of the culture portrays women as sex objects and although women think about sex, they want more than that. They do not want to be used for their bodies. Deep down there is the inner yearning for love, meaningful communication, devotion, and loyalty.

So, they kind of wander around from man to man seeking meaning and not only do they need meaning in a healthy relationship, they need meaning as far as their purpose is concerned. They do not want to be just mothers of a newborn, and that in and of itself is an emotional thing because when they have a child with a man or children with a man they are not always certain about their future with that man...

They worry about finances and if the man they are with is competent enough to raise a child in a lifelong experience with them and sometimes if not most times men don't always step up to the plate the way they would like to but since that have become a parent woman stick with them because they have produced a child with them.

This means that meaninglessness exists in the heart of a woman and they crave significance and importance they do not want to just lay down and have sex with a man and just because a woman has sex with a man it does not mean that she loves him but that she may be seeking to please him when in her heart that are drifting apart because there is no love...

So, meaning is of great importance and if a woman cannot find that in a man she becomes empty and kind of like trying to make relationships work that will never really work to her liking. So discernment is needed on when and how to let go of a relationship that had become involved.

And most men because they have become programmed or taught to not love a woman they enter into relationships with destructive thinking that will manifest shortly after meeting a woman because it is strong within them.

Chapter 18
Wisdom Pearl

What is wisdom? Is it of importance and how so we find it? well for a woman, her wisdom is found in her intuitive abilities, her intuitive abilities are her survival instincts and her innate ability to discern things, and some women have developed these abilities so strongly that they are sharper than other women with these survival skills.

This wisdom pearl is in them. And is sometimes fashioned and formed by pains and losses, all sea pearls are formed by the painful irritations of life so the same it goes for a woman's intuitive ability. Done women are toxic because they have not gotten over an incident or incidents with a man because they are emotional beings if they have not experienced healing thru can carry toxicity into their relationships without ever being ready to embark on a journey with a man in a love relationship.

However, if they can heal it will serve as a template or power base for future decision-making that is in her best interest when coming to a man that she may like or have an interest in. Women are great listeners, yes they communicate verbally and do that well and at a rapidity greater than man and this comes at pubic stages but they also can listen because listening is part of communication - the lost art of communication...

They can pick up on information that others cannot because they are tuned into heart frequency because this is key to their survival and to their well-being as a woman, wife, mother, and daughter.

Wisdom is of important to a woman and she needs to see wisdom in a man so that she can place her confidence in a man and follow his leading if she cannot find wisdom, she becomes the boss by default and serves the role reserved for a man and this is a role she does not want to play but will I'd her man cannot play the position and she will so until another person comes more wise than the man she is with.

Chapter 19
Dreams and a Woman's Role in the World

A woman develops dreams after some time, dreams of her dream house, dreams of a future husband. And dreams of family and a certain lifestyle. However, sometimes her dreams are shattered by the events of life and sometimes she becomes so overwhelmed that she cannot and does not dream again.

The ticket is to be able to dream despite hardship and to be able to adjust your dreams to the season of life you are in. When I was younger I had a group of guys that I was friends with and they were what I called dreamers. They were ambitious and always talking about some project they were working on and I realized that even though they may not fulfill some of those dreams that they tried and tried again until they found their niche ...

The Lord gives dreams, and the Lord can shape a woman's heart to dream. and if she is shattered, he can put back the pieces so they can dream again. A woman's role in the world is lost if she has no ability to dream. I don't care how old she gets if she can dream, she can live an awesome life...

So, it's not about having money, or having the contacts as long as she is in contact with God she has the right contact so that she can dream and see a brighter role in the world, a role that is filled with purpose and aligned with the Stars...

You don't stop dreaming physically until you die, dreams are night visions of the soul and you should not lose vision in the real world. Although this world is rough and cold at times, dreams are still possible, and if she can dream, she can have a purpose...

They say "God bless the child that can hold his own ", I say Good bless the child that can dream over and over again until they find their purpose, until they are aligned with the Stars and have a clear view of heaven and their purpose...

Dreams are spiritual in that they have to do with the inner part of you that is immaterial which is your soul and your spirit... they have to do with your thought life but you can see one's thoughts until they are manifested in one's behavior and action and heard in one's words...

Dream until you can't dream no more, Excel until there is nothing left to do. This is why a woman is on earth to see her ability to dream become powerful.

Chapter 20
Women in Service to the Lord

Women who serve God have an inner beauty that is impeccable, they may not feel secure in themselves and they may struggle to find a significant other that serves God with the zeal that they have for Jesus. However, their spirit is excellent and precious to God...

I find that they are more passionate than some men are because they see Jesus as a husband and not just a religious figure that they have heard of and chosen to believe in. They see Jesus as a husband and themselves as his bride which is what communicated the church should be. Whether they are mainline Protestant or Catholic a woman in service to God is beautiful.

Jesus' ministry was both surrounded by women and supported by women financially and at his death they were present to weep and mourn over him. Sometimes they may feel unattractive because of some defect or inner insecurity but the Lord makes them attractive no matter the height or weight Jesus pure love for them and their love for him gives them the joy they are in search of...

As a God-fearing man, I love godly women they don't have to be perfect but their love for him and his message makes them a ten in my eyes. We are all seeking the Lord or inner power through faith in something. But in Jesus a woman finds purpose and satisfaction that is other worldly. And her mind is wise because she has learned to love wisdom rather than enjoy folly, no matter the age or situation a woman in service to the Lord is non pareil, second to none and there is no other...

I think of most guys were seeking a godly woman they would see life and love different and the creation of women different women would not be abused or used and women would be seen as a gift and not as someone to be mishandled they may know everything but they may love everything about Jesus and that is enough...

It is the person of Christ we should adore and not religion itself although in religion we claim to adore Christ. It is his sacrifice and undeniable reality and love that make par excellence, the cream of the crop. He has been allotted a portion with the great because of the painful sacrifice, and that sacrifice puts a value on women that is Ext ordinaire.

Chapter 21
The Power of Ones Words

Relationships, are filled with conversation. Conversation about money, family, life, and love but one thing we do not realize is the power of one's words in a relationship that can have devastating and long-lasting affects if we are not careful about how we choose them.

I watched my mother as my dad verbally abuses her, constantly putting her down and comparing her to other women. It gads debilitating effects ... Sometimes it was the way he responded to her... Sometimes it was so random that it made the household a constant atmosphere for arguing.

I never liked the arguing and could see how it hurt her... She lived to please him but it was never enough, never ever enough. His words were like a two-edged sword and wielded without thought and concern only the thought of what he could say to belittle her... And sometimes it became apparent that he had an evil spirit.

Words carry creative energy because they come from one's spirit and one's spirit has power. When we have relationships it's all about our speech in the beginning. Our words pull each other in and men say the sweetest things at times just to get close to them and women listen to a man's words to see if she can hear God in them...

If she can't hear God, she won't gather towards him but if she can her defenses come down and she begins to surrender to him. The problem lies with after getting past the preliminary stages of love. And when two people get used to each other. then everything but the kitchen sink gets thrown at the other person...

However, if one can love be your guide then words that are kind won't be hard to come by and that relationship will be made strong and long lasting.

Chapter 22
Drugs and The Ladies

We live in a society that is laced with drugs and I have met women that have had their share of burdens to carry because they fell into the world of active drug use and abuse. In my work in the past with drug treatment I have met many mothers who have been separated from their children because they have spiraled down into the black hole of addiction...

For a woman to carry a child for 9 months of their life, only to lose that child because of a bad decision or bad decisions is soul wrecking and I have seen the tears and the confusion on their faces in the room of an office as they were being interviewed and assessed.

The culture of society is filled with drugs, sex, and music and some of this is a contributing factor of a woman's brokenness. When a woman is broken, she feels as though her life is shattered into a million and one pieces and that to find all the pieces of herself is impossible.

However, if she can find God, she can get the help she needs to take care of her soul in the process. Heroin and fentanyl are the drugs that seem to the most damage something about a needle in the arm shows how low one has become in her thinking and in life...

Sometimes the fathers of their children are on drugs or not in their life to provide support, and sometimes they alternate from men to men, having addictive love affairs that don't last and are without meaning.

The drugs bring out the darkness where inner beauty lies .it seems like both the darkness and beauty are within and the dope brings out the darkness. Some turn to prostitution to make money for their habit... And that propels them into further darkness.

But God... Still can save these women and i have witnessed

miraculous turn arounds where their smile comes back in a genuine way and life back to her eyes and they can dance with life again— keeping in touch with the spirit of things.

Chapter 23
Why the Hummingbird?

The humming bird is an interesting creature. It's very small but very feisty. Its wings flap voraciously when it is in the air and seeking to gather nectar from a flower. And it can cover miles upon miles when navigating the air in search of food. Its babies and nest are very small and we are mesmerized by its various colors...

The hummingbird is God's creation. Unbeknownst to some it has been used as a symbol of love spell in Haitian voodoo and in Latino voodoo known as Santeria. However, it is God's creation first and always will be part of Gods creative order and the hummingbird is symbolic of the angelic and of women who seek the sweetness of life.

It is a fight indeed to seek the sweetness of life. Nothing comes easy and for women the work is ten times harder than it is for a man. A woman is in competition with another woman in how she dresses and looks. A woman plays the role of mother, daughter, sister and lover. And her femininity is of the utmost beauty because God made her that way...

She is not to be toyed with because "hell has no fury like a woman scorned" but if you love her and treat her right then she is the most faithful lover and giver in the world, and when it comes to giving there is no telling what mountain she will move for her beneficiaries because she is the purest benefactor... Pure with love.

The hummingbird is one of many eye candies of the creative order and I chose the hummingbird because of its illustrious beauty. Yet, it's hard for a women to have good self-esteem because of the constant blows to her ego and consciousness come to shatter her feminine frame into oblivion but she is strong and can endure the toughest storms... Because God wired her that way to endure hardship...

No matter the color or culture women everywhere possess their own beauty and she like the humming bird are extremely fierce when it comes to her children. She will go to war for them, and sacrifice herself without hesitation. This is love and this is a picture of the messiah in a feminine way. Because the messiah is described in both masculine and feminine attributes, he is the lion of Judah yet the Lilly of the valley, he is the rose of Sharon yet the king...

In the feminine quality we find God at the pinnacle of parallel and example. To know a women's heart is to know her love for God and to know God is to know the love and value of women... This is the hummingbird in all its radiant colors seeking well concocted nectar from its drooping yet beautiful flowers of choice.

Chapter 24
Celestial Comfort

The word comfort means different things to different people, some find comfort in an alcoholic drink, some find comfort in a fire place, some find comfort in religion and some find comfort in a woman's arms...

It is the nurturing of a woman that brings up children and makes a one room shack a home. Women are nurturers by design. God put that ability in them so that children would have adequate love and care. It come from above.

Of course, there are cases of neglect that we hear about and disregard but for the most part mothers are fierce fighter of their children and fierce lovers as well of them. The term nature vs Nurture are long drawn out in classrooms discussing the psychology of children as it relates to their parents.

In the end, love seems to be the trump card and the gift is from up above, it is ethereal, celestial. It does not mean it is perfect it just means it's from above and God has wired women this way. Nurture is so needed in development of early childhood, from birth it is important that children are held, fed, spoken to with care.

Some may argue that it is not from above. They may argue it is learned behave but it seems to be innate, an in born quality of God that is manifested in the feminine quality of women and women never lose that throughout life, it is always there.

Chapter 25
Fruitful Blessings

Women must discover their purpose, and sometimes it's a difficult process to discover a fulfilling life and contribution to the world and the world around them. Mother hood is not enough although very fulfilling, employment is not enough although it pays the bills, meeting a nice guy who is kind yet strong is not enough...

I think when one discusses person you have to go to the creator for that but if you have no spirituality or religion, it's difficult to approach him, and who is to say which faith is right when there are so many in the world today...

One can look at one's talents and inherent abilities, but how do you apply them to find meaning, is life all about the money? It seems like that most times. I once had a vision of the most juggernaut piece of fruit and I was holding it. I woke up and read john 15 out of the gospels...

At that moment I discovered that the desire of our creator is that we bear fruit, I was going through a hard time at that time and discovered the lords was purging me to bear tremendous fruit, unheard of fruit and the same it goes for the ladies...

The Lord Jesus desires fruit to the father's glory, see because they never will be fulfilled until we learn to participate in the father's glory, which is true glory and last for eternity... Down here on earth things come and go, money comes and goes, friends come and go, and eventually we come and go...

Women are not fulfilled until they bear fruit to the father's glory. And they have to be connected with God for that ... Life is an aimless walk without God!

So, to close all that we discussed in this book out, God is into redeeming eve, redeeming the women, she was betrayed by Satan in the garden of Eden. But Christ wants to redeem eve, he eve who first fell and the eve in every woman because somehow since the fall, eve has put a blemish on all woman but Jesus comes to purge the blemish, remove the blemish from the adamic fall...

Eve wanted knowledge and she wanted to be like God! But she was deceived by the serpent that was more wise than her. And now God is calling all women back to God so that they might find the queen in them and remove the blemish once and for all...

www.ingramcontent.com/pod-product-compliance
Lightning Source LLC
Chambersburg PA
CBHW020344130626
46549CB00003B/1283